Communication and Auditing:

A Step-by-Step Guide

MELANIE MCKAY, PHD
LOYOLA UNIVERSITY NEW ORLEANS

ELIZABETH ROSA, MBA, CPA, CMA
DESALES UNIVERSITY

Editor: Michele Baird
Publishing Services Supervisor: Christina Smith
Manufacturing Supervisor: Garris Blankenship
Project Coordinator: K.A. Espy
Graphic Designer: Krista Pierson
Rights and Permissions Specialist: Kalina Ingham Hintz
Marketing Manager: Sara Hinckley

Copyright © 2003 by Melanie McKay and Elizabeth Rosa

All rights reserved. No portion of this manuscript may be reproduced or utilized in any form or by any means, electronic or mechanical, including photocopying, recording, or by any information storage and retrieval system, without permission in writing from the author, Melanie McKay and Elizabeth Rosa.

ISBN 0-759-31652-X

The Adaptable Courseware Program consists of products and additions to existing Custom Publishing products that are produced from camera-ready copy. Peer review, class testing, and accuracy are primarily the responsibility of the author(s).

COMMUNICATION AND AUDITING

When an independent CPA firm undertakes an audit of a client company, it initiates one of the key communication processes in professional accounting: attesting to the quality of clients' financial information. Because a company might misrepresent its financial information—as a result of error, inadequate internal controls, or even deliberate manipulation of its records—users of that financial information need assurance from a disinterested and qualified monitor that the information accurately reflects the company's financial position.

Assurance Services and the World of Business

A report by an independent CPA firm provides such assurance. In issuing such a report, the CPA firm attests to the fact that the company's records can be relied on and that the company accounts for its business according to proper professional standards. Such communications place public accountants under a great responsibility because in making them, CPAs act as arbiters of financial reliability in the marketplace. The world of business depends on the assurance and attestation services that CPAs provide; every time they render opinions, CPAs put their professional reputations and that of their firms on the line. Moreover, the recent scandals about questionable auditing practices at Enron, WorldCom, and elsewhere make it all the more important that today's auditors can stand with confidence behind the attestations they make.

The Financial Statement Audit

One of the most common and important attestation services is the financial statement audit, the subject of this guide. In a financial statement audit, accountants (typically members of a CPA firm) study a client company's balance sheet, income statement, and statement of cash flows to make a professional judgment about the reliability of these documents. As the result of performing a financial statement audit, the CPA firm offers assurances about these written records to the client company's audit committee, board of directors, shareholders and potential investors, government agencies (such as the SEC), creditors, and customers. Every time an accounting firm gives an unqualified or "clean" opinion on its client's financial statements, it is stating that the company's financial statements are free of material misstatement. It is also attesting to the fact that the company has presented its financial position, results of operations, and cash flows in conformity with generally accepted accounting principles (GAAP), and that the firm has gathered and evaluated evidence in accordance with generally accepted auditing standards (GAAS) in deriving its opinion.

The Importance of Written Records

Generally accepted auditing standards dictate that the accountant's audit work be adequately planned and supervised; that an understanding of internal control be obtained; and that the evidence obtained, auditing procedures applied, and testing performed provide sufficient competent information with which to form an opinion. To provide proof of having audited in accordance with these professional standards, auditors make elaborate written records of the audit procedures they perform to provide documentation and evidence of the tests and evaluations that were conducted. These written records, which include audit engagement letters, planning documentation, audit programs, and audit workpapers, do not merely convey a story of how the audit was conducted but sometimes also serve to protect the accounting firm in liability disputes. Should an accounting firm ever have to defend its audit opinion in a court of law, this documentation would serve as important proof of professional competence and of non-negligent conduct in performing the audit.

Auditing requires adherence to professional auditing standards, hard work, and a thorough understanding of the client's company. This understanding—essential to the audit process—depends on effective oral and written communications among the audit team, between the auditors and the client company, and between the auditors and the parties who will use the client's information. From the accounting firm's initial engagement proposal to its final auditor's report, a successful audit consists of gathering and evaluating evidence within an environment of honest and thorough communication.

COMMUNICATION EVENTS IN THE AUDIT ENGAGEMENT

In this guide, we describe the communication events that typically take place during a financial statement audit. To give you an inside look at what it is like to perform an audit, we have modeled the audit we discuss on one actually performed by an independent CPA firm. By focusing on real-world examples of audit documents, particularly those generated by staff and senior accountants, we introduce you to the kinds of communication skills that are expected of new accountants in the audit field. The exercises at the end of the guide give you the chance to practice and refine those skills.

Communication Events Before and During an Audit Engagement.

1. Once the accounting firm has won the client, a partner, often with assistance from the firm's legal department, prepares an engagement letter. The engagement letter is a contract stating the terms and conditions of the engagement, the services the auditor firm will perform, and the fees that will be charged.

2. After both parties have signed the engagement letter, an audit planning meeting takes place among the engagement partner, the engagement manager (a supervisory-level accountant responsible for managing several concurrent engagements), the audit senior, and the audit staff. At this meeting, the audit team discusses preliminary information gathered from the client and agrees on an audit plan and schedule.

3. Based on discussion at the audit planning meeting, the audit senior writes a planning memo for the engagement. This document formally summarizes planning activities for the engagement and helps members of the audit team to design the audit program.

4. The audit program, which lays out in detail the steps and procedures for the engagement, is either selected from a bank of prewritten programs and tailored to the individual client or is written from scratch to suit the special requirements of the audit about to be undertaken.

5. During all phases of the audit, interviews with the client take place, usually at the client's place of business. Staff and/or senior accountants interview client management and other key employees for information regarding various audit issues.

6. During the course of the audit, audit staff and seniors record the procedures they have performed, the evidence they have gathered, and the conclusions they have reached in the audit workpapers. Writing for the workpapers, the most common type of writing that new auditors do, includes tickmark explanations, descriptive narratives, summaries, and analyses.

7. As the audit draws to a close, the audit staff and senior typically write the management comments, which are descriptions of reportable conditions (significant deficiencies in the design or operation of internal control). After being reviewed by the client and, usually, by the audit manager and audit partner, the management comments are drafted into a formal management comment letter. This letter may also contain the auditor's recommendations for operational improvement.

8. At the end of the audit, the final audit report is compiled. The report usually consists of the auditor's opinion letter, the audited financial statements, and the notes to the financial statements.

As you can see, an audit consists of numerous oral and written communication events and many different types of documentation. There can be a variety of other kinds of communication unique to each audit, of course, and every accounting firm has its own preferred forms of written documentation. We focus in the next section, however, on the communication events you can expect to encounter in any audit (see Figure 1).

A. Engagement Letter
Formalizes Contract Between Firm and Client

B. Initial Meeting with Client
Initiates Planning for the Audit

Figure 1—Communication Events During a Typical Audit

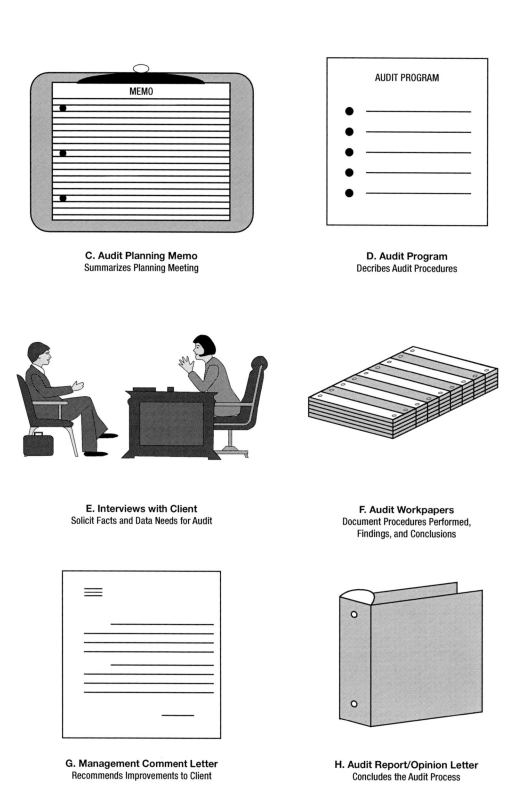

Figure 1 (Continued)—Communication Events During a Typical Audit

The sample documents and descriptions of meetings and interviews in this guide have been derived from communications generated at a large public accounting firm during the audit of a manufacturing company. The audit senior, an accountant in his third year, was responsible for writing many of the original documents. (An audit senior typically performs more complex audit procedures than his staff does and is responsible for supervising the staff accountants assigned to the audit.)

Although more senior members of the firm produced such documents as the engagement letter and the final audit report, staff accountants and seniors were responsible for the communications at the heart of the audit—the agenda for the planning meeting, the planning meeting, the audit planning memo, the client interviews, the workpaper documentation, the management comments, and the management comment letter. Because these communications are among the most important that new accountants are involved in, and because new accountants are often judged by the quality of their communication skills, special care must be taken to ensure that these communication events are carried out in a polished and professional manner.

THE AUDIT ENGAGEMENT LETTER

After the proposal has been accepted, the firm sends the client an engagement letter, spelling out what the firm will do and when, explaining the firm's responsibility for detecting errors and fraud, and confirming fees and billing arrangements. The engagement letter, in reality, is a contract between the accounting firm and the client, and it is always prepared and signed by someone in a position of considerable authority at the firm, usually a partner. Although you will probably not be called on to write an engagement letter during the early years of your career, Figure 2 provides an example of one for your information.

Smith, Williamson, & Walker, LLP
85 Industrial Park Drive
Cincinnati, OH 45210

September 15, 2002

Mr. Chris E. Adams, Controller
Country Crafters, Inc.
636 Apple Street
Glenside, OH 45214

Dear Mr. Adams:

We are pleased to confirm our arrangements with you to audit the financial statements of Country Crafters, Inc., for the year 2002. Ms. Louise Jacobs, partner, will be responsible for the services that we perform for your company.

Figure 2—Sample Engagement Letter

> Our work will consist of an audit of the balance sheet at December 31, 2002, and the related statements of income, retained earnings, and cash flows. The financial statements are the responsibility of the company's management. Our responsibility is to express an opinion on the fairness of the presentation of those financial statements. Our audit will be conducted in accordance with generally accepted auditing standards. Those standards require that we plan and perform our audit to obtain reasonable assurance about whether the balance sheet is free of material misstatement, whether caused by error or fraud. However, because of the characteristics of fraud, particularly those involving concealment and falsified documentation (including forgery), a properly planned and performed audit may not detect a material misstatement. Therefore, an audit conducted in accordance with generally accepted auditing standards is designed to obtain reasonable, rather than absolute, assurance that the balance sheet is free of material misstatement.
>
> An audit includes examining, on a test basis, evidence supporting the amounts and disclosures in the balance sheet. An audit also includes assessing the accounting principles used and significant estimates made by management, as well as evaluating the overall balance sheet presentation.
>
> We will report to the company matters coming to our attention during the course of our audit that we believe are reportable conditions. Reportable conditions are significant deficiencies in the design or operation of internal control that could adversely affect the company's ability to record, process, summarize, and report financial data consistent with the assertions of management in the balance sheet.
>
> Our fee for audit services will be based on our regular per diem rates, plus travel and other out-of-pocket costs. Invoices will be rendered every two weeks and are payable upon presentation.
>
> If you agree with the terms of our engagement described in this letter, please sign the enclosed copy and return it to us. We appreciate the opportunity to be of service to Country Crafters, Inc.
>
> Sincerely,   Accepted by
>
> Smith, Williamson, & Walker, LLP   Chris Adams [client]

Figure 2 (Continued)—Sample Engagement Letter

THE AUDIT PLANNING MEETING

Before the fieldwork begins on an audit engagement, the audit manager and audit partner decide on the overall strategy for the audit and convey these plans to the audit senior. Then they meet with members of the audit team to discuss how the audit will be conducted and to agree on a plan for procedures and scheduling. The audit senior is frequently called on to prepare an agenda for the meeting and, in some cases, might even be responsible for leading the meeting.

Discussion at the planning meeting focuses on specific questions and details of implementation rather than on strategic issues, which have already been decided by senior members of the audit team. Nevertheless, the planning meeting offers staff and seniors a significant opportunity to demonstrate their communication skills and technical knowledge to those members of the firm who will be making crucial decisions about their career advancement. Staff accountants attending the meeting should thoroughly review in advance all preliminary documents, such as the previous years' workpapers, the client's Annual Reports and 10-Ks, accounting guides to the client's industry, FASB statements that might be unfamiliar to the group but relevant to the new client's industry, and so forth. The senior charged with preparing the agenda should think carefully about how the meeting can be most productively organized.

Audit Planning Meeting for Country Crafters, Inc.
October 10, 2002

I. Introduction to Country Crafters, Inc. (Ryan Worthington, audit senior)
   A. Client history
   B. Client's industry environment
   C. Key client management personnel
II. Time frame for the audit (Ryan)
   A. Timing of planning and preliminary fieldwork
   B. Timing of fieldwork and report preparation
   C. Budgeted billable hours for team members
III. Audit objectives and team expectations (Jerry Fields, audit manager)
   A. Audit objectives, materiality, and audit approach
   B. Roles of the audit staff members
   C. Role of the audit senior
IV. Firm's strategy and goals (Louise Jacobs, partner)
   A. Possible problem areas for new client audit
   B. Client's goals and expectations for future business growth
   C. Development of small business advisory services to the client.

Figure 3—Sample Agenda for an Audit Planning Meeting

Note how this agenda structures the time to be spent in the meeting. The audit senior, who is conducting the meeting, begins the meeting by presenting introductory topics himself. He has placed the audit manager's topics in the middle and has reserved the partner's discussion for last. This type of organization for a meeting leads the participants first through a sequence of interesting topics (details on the new client about whom the staff has probably been curious), devotes the middle to mundane but important considerations (scheduling and time constraints), and reserves the most interesting, even engaging topics for the end (discussion of possible problems and of ideas for expanding the firm's services to the client).

The agenda gets the meeting off to an energetic start, allows for some possible waning of interest, but then reenergizes the meeting toward the end. Other meeting strategies are possible, of course, but this strategy is generally reliable, especially for meetings of one hour or less.

THE AUDIT PLANNING MEMO

After the planning meeting takes place, staff or senior auditors may be called on to prepare a planning memo (see Figure 4), a formal written document that summarizes the plan for the audit and dictates to a large extent the content of the audit. To write the planning memo, the audit senior gathers preliminary information such as evaluations of the client's industry, business, and internal control system, results of analytical reviews performed, and assessments of various types of risks to the audit. He then organizes the information in a logical manner so he and his superiors can refer to it easily as they design the appropriate program for the audit.

Planning memos generally contain the following types of information:

- background on the client

- trends within the client's industry

- firm's objectives for the audit

- strategy for the audit

- schedule and timing plans

- synopsized audit program.

Figure 4 is an excerpt from a sample planning memo. Notice how the memo provides essential background information in summary form—that is, in a way that is concise and to the point—and outlines the audit schedule, staffing, and strategy with minimal detail. A more complete plan for the audit will be provided in the audit program.

Country Crafters, Inc.
Audit Planning Memo
For Year Ended December 31, 2002

Client Background and Industry

Country Crafters, Inc., was founded in 1965 by Irene Havice and is a closely held corporation. Irene Havice owns approximately 55% of the company's stock; CEO Mary O'Reilly owns 30%; and Controller Chris Adams owns 1%. The company's other shareholders are various family members or independent small investors, none of whom individually own more than 2% of the company's stock.

As a result of aggressive acquisition of small, family-owned decorative country craft manufacturers, Country Crafters has grown rapidly in the last three years. The company has cornered a niche market in microwaveable pottery cookware and sells these items in national department stores as well as through many nationally distributed decorator housewares catalogs. Aside from the pottery line, which accounts for approximately 30% of the company's annual sales, Country Crafters also produces and sells dolls, toys, furniture, rugs, pillows and throws, jewelry, and clothing.

Audit Objectives

1. Issue the following reports upon completion of our audit:
   • Report on the financial statements
   • Management comment letter
2. Develop Ryan Worthington's skills as an audit senior and provide Kate Larsen and Claire Dufour (staff) with manufacturing audit experience.
3. Improve our firm's relationship with Irene Havice (majority owner) and Mary O'Reilly (CEO) in the interest of expanding our services into a business advisory engagement next year.

Engagement Timing and Staffing

Audit planning	October 15—31, 2002
Interim fieldwork	November 1—5, 2002
Final fieldwork and report preparation	January 15—February 25, 2003
Delivery of annual report and management comment letter	March 21, 2003

Staff		Budgeted Hours
Engagement Partner	Louise Jacobs	40
Engagement Manager	Jerry Fields	80
Engagement Senior	Ryan Worthington	300
Staff	Kate Larsen	200
Staff	Claire Dufour	200

Audit Strategy

To determine the audit strategy, S, W, & W first considered inherent risks to Country Crafters' continuing viability. We considered general economic conditions, relevant technological changes, competition from existing sources, and potential competition from new sources. We found significant risks from domestic competition and from growing markets in Mexico. Both the industry and Country Crafters are profitable, however, and are generating positive cash flows.

We also obtained and reviewed recent financial information for Country Crafters, including the prior

Figure 4—An Audit Planning Memo (excerpted)

years' workpapers (prepared by Henderson and Marks, CPAs). We conducted discussions with Country Crafters' management on matters of internal control.

Country Crafters' management has asked S, W, & W to help it assess the feasibility of opening its own line of retail stores in major shopping malls. During the course of the audit, team members should keep an eye open to any information that might be useful in a management advisory engagement subsequent to the audit.

Audit Program

A detailed audit program has been prepared and approved. The following is an overview of major accounts/audit areas.

Cash

Country Crafters maintains two bank accounts: a major operating account and a payroll account. Confirmations and requests for cutoff bank statements will be sent on both accounts. Returned confirmations will be reviewed against loan agreements, corporate minutes, etc.

We will trace and test prepared-by-client bank reconciliations and investigate interbank transfers.

Inventory

We will observe the client's taking of physical inventory (raw materials, work-in-process, and finished goods).

We will discuss with the client the company's inventory valuation procedures and pricing policies.

We will test the computational accuracy of the client's physical inventory sheets and will review those sheets for individually significant raw material, work-in-process, and finished good items.

Figure 4 (Continued)—An Audit Planning Memo (excerpted)

THE AUDIT PROGRAM

Based on determinations made about the client through the planning process, the audit team supervisors (such as the partner, manager, and, perhaps, the senior) select and/or design an audit program appropriate for the client. The audit program is a detailed set of written instructions that describes the audit procedures and the sequence in which they will be performed. It is an important tool for controlling the progress and quality of the audit because it requires that the team specify the following in writing:

- the overall plan for the work.

- details of required audit procedures, often in the form of instructions for staff accountants working on the audit.

- a means of controlling the time spent on the audit.

- evidence of the work performed on the audit.

Although staff auditors generally do not write these audit programs from scratch, they must be able to understand the technical language used. On occasion, they may be called on to make written modification(s) to existing audit programs. Audit seniors can be expected to write audit programs or parts of them, and these programs are usually evaluated by the audit manager and/or partner. Therefore, certainly audit seniors but even first-year accountants should be able to write clear and concise instructions.

Guidelines for Writing Clear Instructions

1. Use chronological order. Properly written instructions create a step-by-step process for the reader.
2. Number each step clearly. Enumerating what to do first, second, third, and so forth, helps a reader stay on track.
3. Treat closely related actions as a single step.

   Example: Determine which bank accounts need subsequent period cutoff statements and write a letter to the bank(s) requesting that these statements be mailed to our post office box.

   Although this step describes two actions, the second is a direct follow-up to the first and therefore depends on it. Your instructions should clearly indicate this relationship.

4. Use active voice and address the reader directly. Writing directly to your reader makes it easy to keep your directions in the active voice (and therefore clear). Compare these two examples:

   Example: The company's physical inventory should be observed via the firm's separate inventory observation program.

   versus

   Following the firm's separate inventory observation program, observe the company's taking of physical inventory.

   The first sentence, which avoids addressing the reader directly, is impersonal and passive. The second sentence seems much more immediate: "Do this step next."

5. Define any terms that may be unfamiliar to potential readers. Compare these examples:

   Example: Request, review, and summarize the client's IRMQ and compare results with prior years' file information.

   versus

   Request, review, and summarize the client's Insurance Risk Management Questionnaire (IRMQ) and compare results with prior years' file information.

6. Test your instructions by following them yourself. A trial run is the best way of checking your completeness and accuracy. A walk-through will show you immediately where you have left out important information, treated separate elements as single steps, or described procedures vaguely.

Figures 5 and 6 show excerpts from the audit program for Country Crafters. Notice how these instructions follow the guidelines outlined.

Audit Procedures
1. Send 12/31 confirmation requests for each bank account as well as for balances in savings institutions, certificates of deposit, and compensating balances. Use the standard confirmation forms to make these requests. Mail second requests if necessary.
2. Determine which bank accounts need subsequent-period cutoff statements and write a letter to the bank(s) requesting that these statements be mailed to our post office box.
3. Obtain prepared-by-client bank reconciliations and perform the following procedures:
   a. Trace the balance per bank on the reconciliation to the standard bank confirmation form received from the bank.
   b. Trace the balance per books to the general ledger, the trial balance, and the cash lead schedule.
   c. Review cash receipts and disbursements in each bank account for two months prior to and one month after 12/31 and perform other appropriate procedures to identify inter-bank transfer checks and deposits.

Figure 5—An Excerpt from an Audit Program for Cash Audit Procedures

---

Audit Procedures
1. Use the firm's separate inventory observation program to review the company's taking of physical inventory.
2. Test the client's physical inventory sheets for computational accuracy:
   a. Trace counts taken during the physical inventory observation to the physical inventory sheets.
   b. On a test basis, compare tag numbers obtained during the physical inventory observation to those tag numbers noted on the inventory sheets. Investigate any irregular tag references.
   c. Reconcile the physical inventory sheets to the general ledger account balance. Investigate and explain any material discrepancies.
3. Determine the adequacy and appropriateness of allowances for scrap and obsolete inventory items, using the following procedures.

Figure 6—An Excerpt from an Audit Program for Inventory

Audit programs are important to every phase of the audit because they contain the instructions that auditors need to complete the necessary audit procedures and because they document the auditors' compliance with firm and professional standards. As we noted earlier, much of the writing that staff auditors do is in fact to provide verification—in the workpapers—that the audit procedures in the program were performed and to note any reportable conditions (i.e., problems) that were detected.

INTERVIEWS WITH THE CLIENT

One of the auditor's main jobs is to gather thorough and accurate information about the client company's financial practices and systems of control. For this reason, fact-gathering interviews with employees of the client company represent a large part of any audit. Staff and senior accountants routinely conduct these interviews, which can include meetings with everyone from the company's account clerks to its chief financial officer.

Challenges for the Client

The very nature of the audit process can make client interviewing a challenging communication task. It is the auditor's job, after all, to probe into the heart of the client's financial situation, to test systems and identify weaknesses, to review procedures and uncover discrepancies between policy and practice. The auditor must maintain an attitude of skepticism toward all information she receives, withholding judgment about the client's financial information until fieldwork has been completed. In the atmosphere of scrutiny and skepticism created by an audit, potential interviewees may feel defensive and even reluctant to cooperate with the audit team. This reluctance is especially likely among employees who feel uncertain about their job performance or have information they want to hide.

Challenges for the Auditor

Interviews can be intimidating for auditors as well. The new auditor interviewing a chief financial officer, for example, could feel overpowered by the latter's relative maturity and business experience. If, in such a situation, the CFO seemed evasive, the auditor might find it hard to probe as deeply as necessary to uncover all the facts.

Because the relationship between auditor and client is a delicate one, auditors must approach client interviews with sensitivity and flexibility. By doing so, auditors can turn client interviews into an opportunity, not only to gather facts, but also to create a positive working relationship with the client. The following checklist gives you a quick summary.

TIPS FOR SUCCESSFUL CLIENT INTERVIEWING

1. Before meeting with the client, prepare by learning everything you reasonably can about the client's company, its organization, and problem areas.

2. Outline a plan for the interview, organize it by major subjects, and write down detailed questions that you intend to ask about each of those subjects. Use a mixture of open and closed questions to get the client talking but to keep him or her on track.

   Open questions get people talking. They offer respondents the chance to give both broad and in-depth answers. Open questions often begin with the words *how, what, why*, and *where*.

   Closed questions narrow the focus of the interview. Questions that force respondents to choose among two or more possible answers (*yes* or *no, method a, b,* or *c*) are of this type. So are questions that ask for specific information (*names, numbers*). Closed questions often begin with such words as *do you/did you, when, who, how many*.

   Remember: Too many closed questions in a row make an interviewee feel interrogated!

3. Be punctual. Keeping people waiting is not only rude; it also makes them feel put down.

4. Begin the interview with a friendly smile and a firm handshake. Look the interviewee right in the eye. Smiles and straightforward eye contact put people at ease and create a positive first impression.

5. "Break the ice" with a comment on the weather, a sports triumph by the local team, a reference to an object on the interviewee's desk or wall.

6. Begin your interview with the simplest and least sensitive questions. Proceed to the more difficult questions only when your rapport with the client seems well established.

7. Take notes unobtrusively, and write up your notes as soon after the interview as you can.

During the Country Crafters audit, one of the staff auditors, Kate Larsen, became skeptical about the balance in the client's allowance for uncollectible accounts. She had noticed that the balance was distinctly lower than it had been in prior years while the amount of account sales for the year had grown. Her audit senior suggested that she make an appointment to discuss the matter with the company controller, Chris Adams.

Because Kate was aware that the controller might feel defensive during an interview where he would be asked to justify the low balance in the allowance account, Kate planned to make an effort to break the ice before asking any probing questions. She jotted down a few notes with questions she wanted to ask the controller, and then went to his office punctually for the interview.

Kate: Good morning, Mr. Adams. Thank you very much for seeing me today on such short notice.

Chris: No problem, Kate, and please call me Chris. Would you like some coffee?

Kate: Thanks—that would be great. [*Chris pours the two cups of coffee.*] I must tell you that I'm very pleased to have been assigned to your company, Chris. Your company runs well and all your employees have been so helpful and friendly. [*Kate is breaking the ice by paying the company a compliment, and in so doing she indirectly pays Chris a compliment too.*]

Chris: Yes, we've got a great team here in the accounting office. Mary (the CEO) and I try to maintain a family-like atmosphere here in administration, and it seems to be working very well.

Kate: [*Taking her coffee*] Thanks. [*They both sit down.*] Well, let me not take up too much of your valuable time this morning. I have just a few questions I'd like to ask you about the company's receivables. [*Kate shows respect for Chris and his busy schedule by promising to keep the meeting brief.*]

Chris: Sure, go right ahead.

Kate: I've noticed that your sales in general have gone up this year—by the way, that's great!—and that your sales made on account have also gone up, which makes perfect sense. However, I also noticed that the allowance for uncollectibles has gone down as a percentage of year-end receivables. I was wondering about the reasons for this change in company estimates. [*Kate brings up the delicate issue—that the company is making a perhaps overly ambitious estimate of its uncollectible accounts—in a delicate manner: She simply states what she has seen in the accounting records without pointing a finger at the controller, even though he is the person who is probably responsible for making the decision to lower the estimate of uncollectible accounts. She poses the question as an open one, allowing Chris to respond in his own words.*]

Chris: Well, you know, I am not the only one who decides on how to estimate the uncollectibles. The credit manager has a lot to do with it too. [*Chris evades Kate's question somewhat and even sounds a bit defensive.*]

Kate: Yes, I see. It's perfectly logical that he would have a good idea of which customers were good risks and which were not, but I'm sure that you have your own insights into the situation. What is your understanding of the creditworthiness of your customers?
[*Kate probes for Chris's explanation of the allowance.*]

Chris: Well, I do realize that other home decor manufacturers suffer more bad accounts than we do—I think the industry average is somewhere between 2% and 3% of credit sales—but we have very good customers. And some of them have somewhat unusual paying patterns. For example, Natural-Is-Nice, Sugarbox, Hall's, and Southern Style pay their invoices only once a year—in January when all their Christmas cash is rolling in.

Kate: Do you mean that even if they buy merchandise in March, it isn't paid for until the following January? [*Kate makes sure that she has understood his point by turning her question into a restatement of what Chris said. By asking him, in essence, to repeat what he was saying, she keeps him on the subject and gives him a little direction to keep talking about the subject of interest.*]

Chris: That's right—and they always do pay. To my knowledge, none of our major customers are getting ready to go bankrupt and it sure would take a lot of the little guys defaulting to go beyond some $36,000 of allowance! In fact, for the last two years, we have written off less than 1% of our credit sales each year. I think that's pretty good.

Kate: Very impressive, considering what goes on industry-wide. What do you think those other guys are doing wrong? *[Rather than asking Chris to defend his position, and perhaps risk making him defensive, Kate asks Chris for a critique of the company's competitors.]*

Chris: I think many of them do business with little mom-and-pop gift and craft shops. You, know, shops whose owners go into it just for fun without doing their homework. Sometimes a little place like that can come and go in less than a year. We only sell to those places by insisting that they buy on credit cards, like Visa or MasterCard. We just don't take chances with small customers.

Kate: Very interesting. Well, thanks for giving me the scoop on this, Chris. I really appreciate your giving me some of your time.

Chris: Sure. Just let me know if you need anything else. I'll be here.

By relying on open questions in this preliminary interview, Kate has invited the interviewee to give his impressions of the situation in question. Open questions help build trust in audit interviews by encouraging interviewees to give their opinions and insights. Although Kate may still have some unanswered questions, she ends the interview when she is satisfied with the basic information obtained. Realizing that additional auditing work needs to be done to assess the allowance objectively, she politely closes the interview, leaving on good terms with the controller so that future interviews will be productive.

As soon as possible after meeting with the client, the auditor should assemble her notes and draft a memo summarizing the interview. Memos summarizing client interviews are addressed to the audit workpapers (treated in a later section of this guide) and represent important documentation for the audit. Figure 7 illustrates how Kate might document her interview with the controller.

> Date: January 17, 2003
> To: 2002 Audit Workpapers/Country Crafters
> From: Kate Larsen, Staff Auditor
> Subject: Uncollectible Accounts Allowance Determination
>
> On January 16, 2003, I held a discussion with Chris Adams, Country Crafters' controller, about the company's process for determining the Allowance for Uncollectible Accounts so that S, W, & W will be able to assess its adequacy.
>
> The current allowance of approximately $36,000 represents 0.75% of the company's 12/31/02 accounts receivable. This amount is 1.25% lower than the 2% proportion that Country Crafters has historically maintained as its allowance. In addition, the controller has indicated that Country Crafters, for the past two years, has written off, on average, less than 1% of its credit sales. This percentage compares favorably to the norm in the home decor manufacturing industry, which, according to the controller, experiences bad debt write-offs of between 2% and 3% of credit sales nationally.
>
> According to the controller, any customer having a balance in Accounts Receivable as of December 31 can be considered a reliable collection because customers' cash flows are in peak condition during and immediately after the Christmas shopping season, and most customers pay during this time.
>
> The controller is confident that the current allowance of $35,692 is adequate to cover any potential losses. Here are the reasons he cites:
> 1. All of the major customers are paid up and none are in danger of declaring bankruptcy.
> 2. The number of small customers that could default would have to be very large to exceed the $36,000 allowance on the books.
> 3. The Over-90-Days balance appears high because several customers pay invoices only once a year. These customers (Natural-Is-Nice Company, Sugarbox Stores, Hall's Department Stores, and Southern Style Stores) pay their invoices in January regardless of their invoice dates or merchandise receipt dates.
>
> In my opinion, S, W, & W will need to do further testing to assess the adequacy of the allowance for uncollectible accounts and to assess the validity of lowering the balance in the allowance to a smaller percentage of year-end receivables. See workpaper B-25 for further testing.

Figure 7—Sample Memo Documenting Client Interview

In her memo, addressed to the file, Kate is not simply making notes for herself, but creating a record of part of the audit for multiple potential audiences:

1. her audit supervisor, who routinely reviews her work;
2. other members of the audit team, who may want to determine how this interview illuminates other aspects of the audit;
3. members of future audit teams, who may want to review the workpapers from this year's audit before beginning their own;
4. attorneys and/or court officials, should the audit later be subject to litigation by either party involved.

Kate writes up the interview in the form of a short report that summarizes the interview and defends a conclusion. Many brief reports are presented in memo format, and much of the documentation created during the audit falls into this category. Reports should contain the following elements:

- An introduction summarizing the subject, purpose, and occasion of the report along with an explanation of how the report is organized.

- A background description of the problem or situation that the accountant studied.

- An explanation of procedures performed to investigate the situation.

- A conclusion drawn from the application of principles and procedures to the problem or situation.

Let us look briefly at the ways Kate's memo conforms to these guidelines. It introduces the context and purpose of the memo in a one-sentence narration:

Example: *Context:* *[When]* On January 16, 2003, *[Who]* I held a discussion with Chris Adams, Country Crafters' controller, *[What]* about the company's process for determining the Allowance for Uncollectible Accounts . . .

Purpose: *[Why]* . . . . so that S, W, & W will be able to assess its adequacy.

Any reader picking up the file will be immediately oriented to Kate's information.

The next two paragraphs summarize the background needed to support the conclusions the writer will draw at the end of the memo. Paragraph 2 identifies past and present allowances maintained by the company and compares these figures with the industry average:

Example: *[Present data]* The current allowance of approximately $36,000 represents .75% of the company's 12/31/02 accounts receivable.

[Past data] This amount is 1.25% lower than the 2% proportion that Country Crafters has historically maintained as its allowance. In addition, the controller has indicated that Country Crafters, for the past two years, has written off, on average, less than 1% of its credit sales.

[Comparative data] This percentage compares favorably to the norm in the home decor manufacturing industry, which, according to the controller, experiences bad debt write-offs of between 2% and 3% of credit sales nationally.

Other readers of the file need these comparative numbers to determine whether they can accept Kate's conclusions.

Paragraph 3 identifies special circumstances in the case that contribute to the company's confidence in the adequacy of its allowance:

Example: [*Special circumstances*] .... customers' cash flows are in peak condition during and immediately after the Christmas shopping season, and most customers pay during this time.

Paragraph 4 presents the rationale for that confidence by clearly and specifically itemizing the client's reasons for its confidence:

Example: The controller is confident that the current allowance of $35,692 is adequate to cover any potential losses. Here are the reasons he cites:

1. All of the major customers are paid up and none are in danger of declaring bankruptcy.
2. The number of small customers that could default would have to be very large to exceed the $36,000 allowance on the books.
3. The Over-90-Days balance appears high because several customers pay invoices only once a year. These customers (Natural-Is-Nice Company, Sugarbox Stores, Hall's Department Stores, and Southern Style Stores) pay their invoices in January regardless of their invoice dates or merchandise receipt dates.

Notice that Kate takes care to attribute this rationale to the company's controller. At this point, she is not drawing a conclusion herself about the collectibility of these balances; rather, she is documenting the client's position on the issue. A crucial difference exists between reporting the client's opinion on an issue and drawing a conclusion as a member of the audit team. Kate's memo makes that difference clear.

Paragraph 5 presents the writer's judgment about the facts presented:

Example: [*Conclusion*] In my opinion, S, W, & W will need to do further testing to assess the adequacy of the allowance for uncollectible accounts and to assess the validity of lowering the balance in the allowance to a smaller percentage of year-end receivables. See workpaper B-25 for further testing.

Once again, Kate hedges her statement about the allowance with the phrase *In my opinion*, indicating that she is not stating a fact but making a judgment based on the facts she has at the time.

WRITING FOR THE AUDIT WORKPAPERS

Perhaps the most significant writing that staff accountants do involves writing for the workpapers. Whether stored on paper or in electronic files, audit workpapers consist of records of evaluated numerical data and descriptions of procedures performed. Workpapers constitute the heart of the audit because they document the work performed. This documentation helps those who supervise and review the audit team and provides crucial support for the auditor's opinion.

According to Statement on Auditing Standards (SAS) No. 41, entitled "Working Papers," working papers ordinarily should include documentation showing that

a) The work has been adequately planned and supervised . . .
b) A sufficient understanding of the internal control structure has been obtained to plan the audit . . . .
c) The audit evidence obtained, the auditing procedures applied, and the testing performed have provided sufficient competent evidential matter to afford a reasonable basis for an opinion . . . .[1]

In order for workpapers to meet these authoritatively defined criteria, they must contain correct, complete information. They must make their often complicated content clear to any future auditor, providing adequate detail but without using vague or ambiguous language. Workpapers should also be succinct and concise so as not to waste the reader's time or lose the reader in unnecessary verbiage.

Here is an example of appropriate and inappropriate descriptions of findings resulting from the performance of an audit procedure for cash:

Example: *Procedure:* Trace all outstanding checks appearing on a bank reconciliation as of a certain date to checks cleared in the bank statement of the subsequent month.

Inappropriate Description of Findings: Nothing came to my attention as a result of applying the procedure.

Appropriate Description of Findings: All outstanding checks appearing on the bank reconciliation were cleared in the subsequent month's bank statement.

The first description of findings is not a description at all; it is a conclusion drawn by the writer without supporting evidence. The phrases *Nothing came to my attention* and *applying the procedure* do not tell potential readers what steps the writer took to review the reconciliation. They simply ask the reader to take the writer's word for the findings. The second version appropriately describes how the writer reviewed the reconciliation against the later statement, thus providing proper documentation of audit procedures.

Types of Workpaper Writing

Writing for the workpapers takes several forms, the most common of which are *tickmark descriptions, narratives, summaries,* and *analyses of work performed.* Although auditors use these types of documentation in various sequences during the course of the audit, we have presented them here from the simplest type to the most complex.

Tickmark Descriptions of Procedures Performed The term *tickmarks* refers to annotations of the workpapers that auditors use to record their findings as they investigate the client's systems and review the supporting documents. The tickmarks themselves are usually symbols accompanied by brief notations. As they perform tests on their client's accounting data, auditors document, in detail, the procedures they followed by making notations on the various workpaper schedules.

To keep these documents legible, the auditors place tickmarks—usually a number, letter, or symbol—next to the item investigated and keyed to a legend at the bottom of the document or on an attached page. The legend indicates what each tickmark means by providing a brief explanation of what the auditor investigated, what she found, and whether she was satisfied with the information. (Figures 8 and 9 illustrate, respectively, inappropriate and appropriate tickmark explanations and use letters of the alphabet as tickmarks keyed to explanations on a separate page.)

COUNTRY CRAFTERS
WORKPAPER B-25
ALLOWANCE FOR UNCOLLECTIBLE ACCOUNTS

Procedures (from the audit program): S, W, & W will select for testing all customer accounts with balances over $5,000 in the Over-90-Days-Past-Due category to assess collectibility. To determine the adequacy of the client's Allowance for Uncollectible Accounts at December 31, 2002, S, W, & W will judge collectibility by considering discussions with the client, analyses of accounts receivable statistics, and historical trends.

Customer	Over-90 Balance
Natural-Is-Nice Company, Ltd.	16,825.27 (a)
Sugarbox Stores	13,749.76 (b)
Geddes-Markle Stores	23,337.08 (c)
TV Shopping Network	7,049.63 (b)
Hall's Department Stores	14,825.24 (b)
Country Catalogues, Inc.	21,787.22 (d)
Southern Style Stores	22,517.91 (b)
TOTAL	120,092.11

S, W, & W Calculation of Uncollectible Accounts Expected

3% of Over-90 Balances	8,351.55 (e)
3% of 61-90 Balances	24,836.98 (e)
2% of 31-60 Balances	16,797.24 (e)
0.15% of 1-30 Balances	21,777.76 (e)
S, W, & W Expectation	71,763.53
Difference	(36,072.00) (f)
Recorded Balance per client's general ledger	35,691.53 G/L

Tickmark Legend
(a) Long-standing customer with good history. Account currently in dispute. Collection likely.
(b) Long-standing customer. Collection likely.
(c) Account was recently in dispute over customer's double dipping on its discount. Collection is likely.
(d) Account recently negotiated. Collection likely.
(e) 3% of the over-90-day and 61—90-day past-due accounts are thought to be uncollectible; less collectibility will be assumed for accounts that are less overdue, and 100% of current accounts will be presumed collectible.
(f) We feel the client's allowance is understated by about half. We will forward the matter to the Summary of Misstatements as a likely misstatement.

Figure 8—Workpaper Schedule with Inappropriate Tickmark Explanations

> **Tickmark Legend**
>
> (a) According to B. Clayton, Collections, this long-standing customer has a good payment history. This customer changed Accounts Payable managers this year and a dispute arose in which the customer insists that the amount over 90 was wired to Country Crafters; however, Country Crafters never received the money. The matter is being investigated and collectibility is assured due to the long- standing relationship with the customer.
>
> (b) According to B. Clayton, Collections, this is a customer of long standing who has never defaulted on bills. As a result of the size and nature of the customer, this customer has the clout to fall delinquent occasionally in paying their bills. They always pay, however, and are expected to pay this over-90 balance as well.
>
> (c) According to B. Clayton, Collections, this matter was recently in dispute. Country Crafters believed that Geddes-Markle was "double dipping" on their discount. Geddes-Markle disagreed, and stopped paying bills while the question was in dispute, thus creating an overdue balance. Geddes-Markle has since admitted that it has been double dipping on its discounts, and payments have resumed with collectibility appearing apparent.
>
> (d) According to B. Clayton, Collections, Country Crafters has had problems with this customer paying by the due date. It appears that terms have been worked out and repayment will occur. Clayton speaks with Country Catalogues on a daily basis and feels that collectibility is likely.
>
> (e) Based on this analysis, 97% of over-90-days-past-due accounts are thought to be collectible. S, W, & W will estimate that the remaining 3% of the over-90-day balance is uncollectible. Additionally, we will assume that 3% of the 61-90-day balance is uncollectible, that 2% of the 31-60-day balance is uncollectible, that 0.15% of the 1-30-day balance is uncollectible, and that 100% of current accounts is assumed to be fully collectible. S, W, & W will use such percentages in developing our expectation of the Allowance for Uncollectible Accounts.
>
> (f) The client's write-offs of uncollectible accounts, as well as its sales made on account, appear to have been decreasing in the past few years. For this reason, a decrease in the Allowance for Uncollectible Accounts appears to be warranted. However, the allowance as it currently stands in the client's books represents a disproportionately small percentage of the actual bad debt write-offs that occurred during 2002. We believe that our estimate, as calculated above, of approximately $72,000 would be a better reflection of potential future write-offs. Because the $36,072 difference between the client's estimate and that of S, W, & W is considered to be material, the matter will be forwarded to the Summary of Misstatements (Workpaper #I-5) as a "likely misstatement."

Figure 9—Tickmark Legend with Appropriate Tickmark Explanations

Tickmark explanations must be concise because the space available for them is often limited. They must be complete, however, and able to stand alone as substantive messages. Members of the audit team should not need to consult other documents or ask for clarification to understand the tickmark explanations on a workpaper.

In Figures 8 and 9, staff auditor Kate Larsen has performed substantive testing to determine whether the client's Allowance for Uncollectible Accounts is adequate. As the auditor investigated each past-due customer account, she made a tickmark next to each account.

In the first sample, Figure 8, Kate records the conclusions she reached without specifying what she found. These "explanations" are not really explanations at all, but opinions about the collectibility of certain accounts that the auditor asks her readers to accept on faith. Readers of these documents will have to consult with the writer about details.

In Figure 9, however, the auditor explains in the tickmark legend exactly what she did and what she discovered as she reviewed each account. Tickmarks (a) through (d) describe the probable collectibility of specific accounts and the reasons for the auditor's assessments. Her explanations appropriately attribute evaluations of the customer to the client (B. Clayton). In tickmarks (e) and (f), the auditor describes details of the calculations she performed to come up with her own estimate of uncollectible accounts and explains why she thinks that the client's estimate is inadequate, considering current circumstances and trends.

Notice in (f) that the auditor has concluded that an item in the client's books (the Allowance for Uncollectible Accounts) may be in dispute and that the finding is carried forward to a more prominent summary worksheet. No doubt the audit senior and possibly even the manager and/or partner will review the summary worksheet; therefore, it is essential that the staff auditor make a clear and accurate record of what she has done and found.

Narrative Documentation of Operational Areas and Internal Control Testing

Narratives are descriptive accounts that document the auditor's investigation of the client's systems, how they are working, which key employees are performing which tasks, and how information is being processed. This documentation helps the auditor understand the functional areas he will be auditing and identify any areas of weak internal control that need consideration.

Narratives describe events in chronological order, explaining each step before moving on to the next. This sequential order makes documentation easy to follow because it presents the tasks in the order in which they were performed. A well-written narrative is like a "flowchart in prose"—easy to follow, with each step clear.

The narrative in Figure 10 describes operational procedures within Country Crafters' purchasing and accounts payable departments. It is typical of the documentation involved in the internal control portion of an audit. To begin a study of a client's internal control system, an auditor questions personnel, prepares internal control questionnaires to identify problem areas, and creates flowcharts depicting duties and functions of key personnel in various functional areas. When he has gathered his information, the auditor writes a narrative describing how the systems operate. Notice that the writer here has used chronological order to describe the purchasing and accounts payable systems and has presented his material using concrete detail.

> **COUNTRY CRAFTERS**
> **SYSTEMS DOCUMENTATION OF**
> **PURCHASING AND ACCOUNTS PAYABLE**
> **2002 AUDIT ENGAGEMENT**
>
> Any company employee may fill out a purchase requisition; however, all purchase requisitions must be approved by department supervisors. Once the requisition is approved, the white and pink copies are forwarded to the Purchasing Department and the yellow copy is maintained by the requisitioner.
>
> The purchase requisition is filed in the Purchasing Department and entered by the purchasing clerk into the computerized accounting system, which creates a purchase order. The purchasing clerk prints out three hard copies of the purchase order: One copy is retained by Purchasing (in addition to the record that is maintained on the computer system), one copy is sent to the accounts payable clerk (pending receipt of goods), and one copy is sent to Receiving, a central facility where the majority of raw material shipments are delivered.
>
> The receiving clerk compares quantities received to quantities ordered and notes any differences. Goods are forwarded with the annotated purchase order to the originator of the purchase requisition, who examines the goods and determines if they are acceptable. If no problems are noted, the originator of the purchase requisition signs the annotated purchase order and forwards it directly to Accounts Payable, with authorization to forward the invoice for payment. Simultaneously in Receiving, a receiving report is prepared and sent to the accounts payable clerk. The accounts payable clerk matches the invoice she received from the vendor to the original purchase order, the annotated purchase order, and the receiving report, and posts the transaction to the accounts payable ledger.
>
> Any significant differences between purchase orders and invoices are brought to the attention of the purchasing clerk, who is responsible for investigating differences and coming to a reasonable compromise or solution with the vendor. If all supporting documentation has been collected and if there are no unresolved significant differences between the purchase order, annotated purchase order, receiving report, and invoice, the accounts payable clerk sends the invoice, with authorization for payment, as it becomes due to the Treasurer's Office for payment.

Figure 10—Sample Workpaper/Narrative

Summaries of Tests Performed Once the auditor has fully understood and documented the operating procedures of the functional area under study, he begins performing tests of that area's internal controls to see if, in fact, the area is operating as it is supposed to. Of course, the auditor must document the testing he performs by describing what he did and any conclusions about the client's internal controls that he reached. The form of this internal control documentation can vary from firm to firm, but proper documentation always includes a description of the internal control in question and a summary of test(s) performed, along with the auditor's conclusion about the quality of that control.

The difference between summary documentation and narrative documentation rests primarily in the level of detail involved. Whereas narratives describe each step in a process, a series of procedures, or a chain of events, summaries highlight important information to give a general picture of events and actions. The summaries in the workpaper in Figure 11 (from the Country Crafters audit) illustrate the point. Rather than describing each test performed, the summaries explain in each case how the whole testing process was conducted. What emerges is not a set of discrete, specific descriptions, but a generalization about the effectiveness of the company's internal controls.

> **COUNTRY CRAFTERS**
> **TESTING OF INTERNAL CONTROL: PURCHASING**
> **2002 AUDIT ENGAGEMENT**
>
> **Desirable Control:** Bank reconciliations are performed on a monthly basis.
>
> **Test of Control:** S, W, & W tested this control by examining monthly reconciliations of the operating bank account. S, W, & W noted that each reconciliation was completed by the staff accountant on a timely basis. In addition, each reconciliation was reviewed and approved by the accounting manager on a timely basis. Based on a discussion with the accounting manager, S, W, & W noted that all monthly bank reconciliations are reviewed for accuracy, completeness, and timeliness.
>
> **Conclusion:** Based on testing performed, this control appears to be functioning as intended and, therefore, contributing to the reliability of the purchasing, accounts payable, and cash disbursements systems.
>
> **Desirable Control:** Periodic comparisons are made of actual expenses to budgeted expenses by the vice president of administration.
>
> **Test of Control:** Based on an interview with the VP of administration and his staff, S, W, & W noted that comparisons of budgeted to actual expenses are performed periodically throughout the year. Accounts where actual expenses exceed budgeted amounts are investigated. In such instances, the VP of administration informs the appropriate department head of the situation and asks the department head for an explanation of the overage. In addition, the VP of administration reminds the department head that a budget transfer request should be prepared and submitted. Because of these periodic reviews and discussions with department heads, the VP of administration is able to identify problems that arise within departments purchasing raw materials as well as possible accounting errors/irregularities within the related purchasing accounts.
>
> **Conclusion:** Based on testing above, it appears that this control is in effect and operating as intended.
>
> **Desirable Control:** Purchase requisitions are approved by applicable department supervisor.
>
> **Test of Control:** S, W, & W randomly selected 200 executed purchase requisitions from the file in the Purchasing Department and noted the applicable approval signature on each form. In a discussion with the purchasing manager (who supervises the purchasing clerk), it was noted that no purchase requisition is entered into the system as a purchase order without the appropriate approval signature.
>
> **Conclusion:** Based on testing above, it appears that this control is in effect and operating as intended.

Figure 11—Sample Workpaper/Summary

Analyses of Work Performed After auditing each account, the auditor writes a memo to the file much like the one you saw in Figure 7 by Kate Larsen summarizing her client interview. The memos discussing account audits, however, focus on the quantitative data obtained, analyze any internal control issues raised from the audit, and offer the auditor's opinions on those issues. Although these memos often include sections of narration and summary, their function is specifically analytical; that is, they are written to discuss an issue raised by the facts of the audit in light of authoritative sources such as FASB Statements of Financial Accounting Standards (SFAS) and AICPA Statements of Position (SOP). It is important to note in these memos any problems encountered during the audit and to provide clear references to supporting documentation such as spreadsheets and references to relevant authority.

In Figure 12, the auditor analyzes whether Country Crafters has properly disclosed several related-party transactions. Statement on Auditing Standards No. 45[2] provides guidelines for identifying and disclosing transactions with entities defined as "related parties" under FASB SFAS No. 57[3]. These guidelines include requesting from client management the names of all related parties, interviewing management about transactions with these parties, reviewing the prior years' workpapers for the names of known related parties, and identifying evidence of related-party transactions in various audit documents. Notice that the writer begins by establishing the authoritative source (SAS 45) she followed in conducting her audit procedures as well as the source (SFAS No. 57) on which she based her analysis.

Date: January 31, 2003

To: 2002 Audit Workpapers
From: Claire Dufour
Subject: Identification of Related Parties

In accordance with SAS 45, S, W, & W has considered related-party transactions and relevant disclosures. To identify related parties and related-party transactions, as they are defined in SFAS No. 57, S, W, & W held discussions with the company president, reviewed the prior year auditor's report, and used knowledge gained throughout the course of the audit. The following related parties were discovered:

Mary O'Reilly   CEO
Amelia Strong   Production Coordinator/CEO's daughter
John O'Reilly   Director of Trademarking/CEO's son
Magda Sullivan   CEO's mother

Corporate Real Estate, Ltd.: Affiliated Entity owned 98% by Amelia Strong and John O'Reilly; 2% by Mary O'Reilly

Omega, Inc.: Affiliated Entity owned 98% by Amelia Strong and John O'Reilly; 2% by Omega L.P.

Omega L.P.: Affiliated Parent Company of Omega, Inc., owned 100% by Magda Sullivan

RELATED-PARTY TRANSACTIONS

S, W, & W identified the following related-party transactions during 2002:

1. Note Receivable from Omega, Inc.
   In connection with a purchase of equipment by Omega, Inc., Country Crafters paid $100,000 on Omega's behalf to the equipment supplier. The note is non-interest bearing and will be paid in full by September 2003.
2. Note Receivable from Corporate Real Estate, Ltd.
   In connection with the purchase of a building by Corporate Real Estate, Ltd., Country Crafters paid $938,682 on Corporate's behalf for the purchase of and renovations to the building. Country Crafters will lease the building from Corporate Real Estate, Ltd., for its new corporate headquarters. This note is non-interest bearing and will be paid in full by June 2006.
3. Stockholder/Officer Loan
   Mary O'Reilly, CEO and 25% stockholder of Country Crafters, advanced $450,000 to the company. The loan is being administered by First National Bank. Annual principal payments are due on May 31 each year in the amount of $45,000 with interest payable monthly at 9%.

Given the nature of the above-described loans, in our opinion, full and adequate disclosure of these related-party transactions has been made by the client in the notes to the financial statements.

Figure 12—Sample Workpaper/Analytical Memo

After establishing the authorities for her investigation, the auditor summarizes the methods used to identify related parties ("held discussions with the company president, reviewed the prior year auditor's report, and used knowledge gained throughout the course of the audit") and identifies the transactions discovered. Because the audience for this workpaper is confined to experts—other auditors and possibly attorneys—the writer does not need to discuss in detail how SAS 45 and SFAS 57 apply to the facts of this audit situation.

Other auditors—familiar with SAS 45 and with SFAS 57—will know what defines a "related party" and will quickly see that the writer used appropriate procedures to identify them in this case. Attorneys reviewing this workpaper in litigation would have to research the relevant authorities as part of the case preparation. Therefore, the writer can, without extensive explanation, draw the conclusion that "full and adequate disclosure" has been made.

The Audit Workpaper Review Process

In a typical accounting firm hierarchy, staff accountants' workpapers are subject to review by the audit senior. The writing of audit seniors is subject to review by the audit manager and often by the audit partner. To make your writing better able to stand up to a supervisor's scrutiny, here are a few suggestions:

Familiarize yourself thoroughly with the style, structure, and conventions of your firm's workpapers and other documents. Studying these documents will give you an idea, in most cases, of what the firm considers to be model documents and what your supervisors expect of your writing.

As you review the documents, ask yourself these questions:

- Who is/are the audience(s) of this document?

- What is its primary purpose? Secondary purpose?

- Have I adopted the appropriate tone for this audience and purpose?

- Have I organized the material in the most effective way?

Always allow time for revising and editing whatever you draft. Revising and editing are key steps in the writing process. Submitting unrevised drafts is a surefire way to stop your career advancement in its tracks.

Remember: Strong, clear writing reflects strong, clear thinking. Both will be noticed, appreciated, and rewarded.

MANAGEMENT COMMENTS AND THE MANAGEMENT COMMENT LETTER

During and after the audit fieldwork, staff auditors are expected to write *management comments,* or descriptions of *reportable conditions* that they observed during the audit. Reportable conditions are defined by the AICPA as "matters coming to the auditor's attention that, in his judgment, should be communicated to the audit committee because they represent significant deficiencies in the design or operation of the internal control structure, which could adversely affect the organization's ability to record, process, summarize, and report financial data consistent with the assertions of management in the financial statements."[4]

A management comment letter to a client's audit committee or board of directors simply communicates any reportable conditions detected during the audit. However, auditors will often write directly to the company's management as well, including in this second version of the management comment letter suggestions for improvement to the client's internal control system and/or to business operating methods. We focus in this section on the type of letters written to a client's management because these letters present particular rhetorical challenges: They must point out the client's areas of weakness and at the same time motivate the client to make improvements. If these comments are written carelessly, they may offend the client and fail to achieve their purpose.

Moreover, well-written management comments can create an opportunity for the audit firm to provide value-added services to the client and, possibly, to develop further business as a result. For all of these reasons, management comments should be drafted with great care.

Tact and Thoroughness

Like audit interviews, management comments are communication tasks requiring sensitivity on the one hand and thoroughness on the other. Well-written management comments describe the problem accurately, but do so in a way that identifies solutions. They emphasize the positive effects that a solution will bring as well as the consequences that will ensue if the problem is ignored. They motivate management to initiate change by presenting the situation clearly and logically. They never use 'finger-pointing' phrases or accusatory language. Obviously, writing effective management comments is a tricky business! With practice, however, you can master this important skill.

Here is an example of a poorly written management comment, along with a revised, improved version:

Poorly written comment
Finding: Our investigation revealed that GeoCorp does not summarize customer return credits. The lack of a summary makes it difficult to monitor the propriety of credits issued or the existence of performance problems with a particular product line. Furthermore, an evaluation cannot be readily performed at the end of each period to ensure that sales and profits are not overstated due to significant returns in the following period.
Recommendation: Monthly, or at a minimum, quarterly, GeoCorp should generate a report listing credits to assist management with monitoring sales returns. In addition, a review of credits issued should be performed quarterly to prevent overstatement of profits.

Improved comment
Observation: GeoCorp processes customer return credits without summarizing them. Regular summaries of these credits would help the company make better decisions about issuing credits and monitor performance problems with particular product lines. In addition, regular summaries would allow the company to evaluate performance at the end of each period to ensure accurate statements of sales and profit.
Management action: Issuing a regular report (monthly or quarterly) listing credits issued would help management monitor sales returns. Conducting a quarterly review of credits issued would help ensure that sales and profits are accurately stated.

Let's compare the two versions to see why the revised comment is more effective than the original.

Connotative Language

In the original comment, the writer uses the label "*Finding*" to introduce the item under discussion: This word suggests that the auditor had to ferret out the truth about the situation rather than simply learn about it from the client. In addition, the writer's language suggests that GeoCorp was trying to hide something from the audit team: "*Our investigation revealed that GeoCorp does not summarize customer credit returns.*" In the revised comment, the label "*Observation,*" along with the straightforward statement of the problem ("*GeoCorp processes customer credit returns without summarizing them*") avoids these negative implications.

Positive vs. Negative Language

The original comment relies on negative words and phrases to express the central idea: "*GeoCorp does not summarize customer credit returns. The lack of a summary . . . an evaluation cannot be readily performed at the end of each period to ensure that sales and profit are not overstated due to significant return in the following period.*" Not only does this language increase the difficulty of the passage but it also produces a condemnatory tone. The revised comment is couched, for the most part, in positive language ("*Regular summaries of these returns would help the company make better decisions about issuing credits and monitor performance problems with particular product lines. In addition, regular summaries would allow the company to evaluate performance at the end of each period to ensure accurate statements of sales and profit*").

The label "*Recommendation*" in the original version, along with the bossy language ("*at a minimum, quarterly, ... should generate a report . . . . a review of credits issued should be performed quarterly*"), could well put the reader on the defensive. The phrase "*to prevent overstatement of profits*" might further antagonize the reader, suggesting as it does that the company may be deliberately trying to overstate profits.

In the revised version, the label "*Management action*" implies that management has already planned to correct the situation and fully intends to do so. The phrasing of the recommendation here sounds more like a gentle suggestion than an order: *Issuing a regular report (monthly or quarterly) listing credits issued would help management monitor sales returns. Conducting a quarterly review of credits issued would help ensure that sales and profits are accurately stated.*

The differences between these "before-and-after" comments may seem subtle, but they will result in real perceptual differences for the reader, differences that will make an impact on how the advice will be received.

Review of Management Comment Letter

When all the management comments are in, they are compiled and edited, usually by the audit senior, into the management comment letter, which formally notifies the client of reportable conditions found during the audit and offers suggestions for improving them. The letter is reviewed by the audit manager and ultimately the audit partner before it is sent to the client; therefore, its writer is under much scrutiny from superiors.

Figure 13 provides a sample management comment letter. Notice that the letter begins with some rather formal language about reportable conditions (paragraph 1). Although management comment letters should be written in the most positive manner possible, such authoritative language should be included because it is required by SAS No. 60. Following the necessary opening, the writer has organized the letter by describing the reportable conditions (the items of greatest significance) first and by listing operational recommendations afterward, in a descending order of importance. Also notice that the writer of the letter incorporated strategies to make points gently and to avoid a critical tone. Tact and proper organization are the keys to writing a management comment letter that will get the points across while fostering positive client relations.

Smith, Williamson, & Walker, LLP
85 Industrial Park Drive
Cincinnati, OH 45210

March 21, 2003

Mr. Chris Adams, Controller
Country Crafters, Inc.
636 Apple Street
Glenside, OH 45214

Dear Mr. Adams:

In planning and performing our audit of the financial statements of Country Crafters, Inc. for the year ended December 31, 2002, we considered its internal control structure in order to determine our auditing procedures for the purpose of expressing our opinion on the financial statements and not to provide assurance on the internal control structure. However, we noted two matters involving internal control and its operation that we consider to be reportable conditions under the standards established by the American Institute of Certified Public Accountants. Reportable conditions involve significant deficiencies in the design or operation of internal control that, in our judgment, could adversely affect the company's ability to record, process, summarize, and report financial data consistent with the assertions of management in the financial statements.

I. Reportable Conditions

<u>Segregation of Duties</u>

A basic element of the internal control structure is adequate segregation of duties. However, given the size of Country Crafters, Inc., segregation of duties among authorization, recording, and custody of assets is not always possible. Currently, one employee is responsible for opening mail, posting receipts to customers' accounts, preparing deposit slips, and making deposits at the bank. The company could achieve the proper segregation of duties by reassigning job responsibilities among other team members. We will be pleased to discuss with you our ideas for how to resolve this problem efficiently and economically.

<u>Written Procedures for Disposal of Fixed Assets</u>

No written procedures exist to inform employees of the necessary steps to be taken upon the disposal of a fixed asset. Disposals without the notification of accounting personnel could result in an overstatement of fixed assets and depreciation expense.

Figure 13—Sample Management Comment Letter

> The company could achieve better control over fixed asset purchases and disposals, improved accountability, and more accurate financial record keeping by limiting authorization for disposals of fixed assets to supervisors. To implement a procedure for such limitation, the company could create a form to list the disposal date, asset description, area, and tag number; supervisors disposing of fixed assets could route the form to accounting, who, in turn, could remove the fixed asset and the related accumulated depreciation from the books.
>
> **II. Recommendations for Operational Improvement**
>
> The following comments are intended to improve your internal structure or to result in other operating efficiencies.
>
> (1) Procedures Manual
>
> The company does not have a formal procedures manual. By developing a written manual, you could ensure that transactions be treated in a standardized manner and that proper internal controls exist. A manual may also reduce the amount of training time necessary for new team members.
>
> (2) Update of Computer Systems
>
> Consider replacing your current computer system with a new general ledger package containing an integrated accounts receivable and payable module. In addition, we suggest keeping the customization of new software to a minimum. Custom software increases the cost of new-technology upgrades.
>
> (3) Production Capacity
>
> Your two current suppliers may not have the capacity to handle the increased volume you anticipate with the growth projected in your business plan. Moreover, the projected growth could create real problems if one or both of your plants should be unable to produce to meet demand. Contracting with a third mill could help you handle the increased volume that you anticipate.
>
> This report is intended solely for the information and use of the board of directors and management within the company.
>
> Sincerely,
> Smith, Williamson, & Walker, LLP

Figure 13 (Continued)—Sample Management Comment Letter

THE AUDIT REPORT

The audit concludes with an audit report, comprising the final set of documents produced by the audit team. The audit report contains, in addition to the audited financial statements themselves, an opinion letter stating whether or not the financial statements of the audited company fairly present the financial situation of the company. The language of the audit opinion letter is largely dictated by the AICPA and depends on what type of opinion the audit firm is rendering. Staff auditors usually do not participate in the writing of the opinion letter. Examples of a standard audit opinion letter and of the possible variations can be found in any auditing textbook. For your immediate information, Figure 14 illustrates a standard audit opinion letter.

> **Smith, Williamson, & Walker, LLP**
> 85 Industrial Park Drive
> Cincinnati, OH 45210
>
> To the Board of Directors of Country Crafters, Inc.:
>
> We have audited the accompanying balance sheet of Country Crafters, Inc., as of December 31, 2002, and the related statements of income, retained earnings, and cash flows for the year then ended. These financial statements are the responsibility of the company's management. Our responsibility is to express an opinion on these financial statements based on our audit.
>
> We conducted our audit in accordance with generally accepted auditing standards. Those standards require that we plan and perform the audit to obtain reasonable assurance about whether the financial statements are free of material misstatement. An audit includes examining, on a test basis, evidence supporting the amounts and disclosures in the financial statements. An audit also includes assessing the accounting principles used and significant estimates made by management, as well as evaluating the overall financial statement presentation. We believe that our audit provides a reasonable basis for our opinion.
>
> In our opinion, the financial statements referred to above present fairly, in all material respects, the financial position of Country Crafters, Inc., as of December 31, 2002, and the results of its operations and its cash flows for the year then ended in conformity with generally accepted accounting principles.
>
> Smith, Williamson, & Walker, LLP
> March 21, 2003

Figure 14—A Standard Audit Opinion Letter

Although the wording of the audit opinion letter is specified by the AICPA, these letters are nevertheless important as the primary means of communicating the auditors' opinion about the credibility of a client's financial statements.

CONCLUSION

The communication events described in this guide do not merely support the financial statement audit; they actually play a large part in creating it because it is the communications that generate the plan, solicit the information the auditors need, document the work performed, and formulate the conclusions. From beginning to end, from client interviews through workpaper documentation to the management comment letter, the communication skills of the audit team will determine the success of the audit.

NOTES

[1] American Institute of Certified Public Accountants, Working Papers, Statement on Auditing Standards No. 41, AU section 339 (New York: American Institute of Certified Public Accountants, 1982).

[2] American Institute of Certified Public Accountants, Related Parties, Statement on Auditing Standards No. 45, AU section 334 (New York: American Institute of Certified Public Accountants, 1983).

[3] Financial Accounting Standards Board, Related Party Disclosures, Statement of Financial Accounting Standards No. 57 (Stamford, CT: Financial Accounting Standards Board, 1982).

[4] American Institute of Certified Public Accountants, Communication of Internal-Control-Structure-Related Matters Noted in an Audit, Statement on Auditing Standards No. 60, AU section 325 (New York: American Institute of Certified Public Accountants, 1989).

EXERCISES

1. **Scenario:** Mark O'Brien, the audit senior on an upcoming assignment, has asked you to help develop an agenda for the audit planning meeting for Fleet Technologies, which will be held on May 5, 2003. He has left a few sketchy notes on your desk listing briefly the topics to be covered in the meeting as well the people who will be responsible for presenting the information.

   Meeting Participants
   Jim Avakean, partner
   Evan Roy, audit manager
   Mark O'Brien, audit senior
   Eileen Wood, staff accountant

   Topics to Be Addressed
   - Firm issues: increased competition, revenue growth risks, and new business areas
   - Audit issues: client industry, potential audit problems
   - Scheduling: interim, year-end, report date
   - Staffing: team work, assignments, expectations
   - Client information: history, management personnel
   - Miscellaneous: time budget, materiality.

   Writing task
   a. Formalize the notes into a meeting agenda that will be sent to the audit staff, senior, and partner on the engagement.
   b. Write a memo to your supervisor, Mark O'Brien, justifying how you organized the agenda.

2. **Scenario:** Your firm has just accepted an audit engagement with a large publicly held company, which, for this assignment, you may choose. Obtain the most recent SEC 10-K filing for this publicly held company using the SEC's EDGAR database on the World Wide Web.

   Writing task: After reading the document carefully, prepare the "Client Background and Industry" portion of the planning memo for the working papers. Comment on any possible audit issues you discover in your research, including lawsuits, significant industry events, emerging technologies, economic factors, or other situations related to the company you have chosen.

3. **Scenario:** The following instructions are excerpts from an audit program that will be used by a first-year staff accountant to perform substantive tests of sales and accounts receivables balances.

   - Confirm AR.
   - Perform alternative procedures for confirmations not returned.
   - Perform analytical procedures to test sales and AR.
   - Trace the AR aging schedule to the ledgers.
   - Perform a sales cutoff test.
   - Verify mathematical accuracy of the AR aging schedule.

   Writing task
   a. Write a memo to the audit team critiquing the audit program steps just listed.
   b. Revise the audit program steps by rewriting them, reordering them, and/or combining them, as needed. Make up any additional information you feel is necessary to make the explanations clear and understandable.

4. **Scenario:** You are a staff accountant auditing the books of a small, privately owned business. During the audit of the cash account, you examined the backs of several canceled checks and noticed some striking similarities in the handwriting of three different endorsers. In addition, you found several unexplained reconciling amounts on the bank reconciliation. You suspect there may be some fraudulent handling of cash in the company. After some discussion with the senior on the job, you have decided to speak to the client's controller about the apparent discrepancies and have come up with the following list of questions.

   - Why is there an unexplained difference between the general ledger balance and the bank account balance?
   - Who routinely prepares the bank reconciliation?
   - Who handles cash disbursements?
   - Are all vendor invoices reviewed and approved prior to payment? By whom?
   - Are the reconciliations reviewed after they are prepared?
   - If reconciliations are reviewed, why were the unexplained differences not resolved properly?
   - Has anyone been fired from the company for stealing?
   - How many vendors have complained about incorrect balances in their accounts?

Writing task: Create a written plan for the interview that answers these questions:
a. What are the goals of the upcoming interview?
b. What risks are involved in the upcoming interview?
c. Which questions should not be asked or should be revised to be less inflammatory?
d. How could some of these questions be rephrased or grouped to streamline the interview and give the manager greater opportunity to respond?
e. Prepare a revised listing of questions in the order you would ask them. Include any additional comments or questions you would use to start and end the interview.
f. Explain the reasoning behind your choices in answering question (e).

5. **Scenario:** Linda Davis is a first-year staff auditor working on her first audit. Unfortunately, over the course of the first two weeks, she has managed to annoy the client's controller, Amy Walters, on more than one occasion. On Monday, Linda asked one of Amy's staff for help in obtaining some files. Proper procedure requires, however, that all requests be directed to the controller. As a result of Linda's unintentional gaffe, Amy barged into the conference room, where the entire audit team was working, to criticize Linda for her actions. The audit team sat in silence as Amy left the room and Linda attempted to continue functioning after the outburst.

Over the following days, Linda made every attempt to avoid contact with Amy. However, on Wednesday, Linda was given a list of follow-up questions by the engagement partner, Jim Fallen, who had reviewed her working papers. She was given until Monday morning of the following week to prepare write-ups for the outstanding issues. Despite this deadline, Linda has put off meeting with Amy, fearing another unpleasant confrontation. The following conversation took place between Linda and Amy at 4:45 p.m. on Friday afternoon.

Linda: [Arriving unexpectedly and entering without being asked] Hi, Amy. I know it's getting late, but I have a few questions to ask you.

Amy: [While straightening up her desk for the day] Oh. OK. I have a few minutes. What's up? [Amy is shuffling papers and stuffing them into her briefcase.]

Linda: Well, I tried to get here earlier but I got bogged down on this one account. Anyway, I'm a little unclear about the company's policies and procedures for issuing credit memos. Could you review them with me?

Amy: [Listening to her voice mail] Hmmm. Credit memos. Well, nothing's changed since last year. You should have something about that in your prior year's workpapers. [Pauses while she listens to a message]

Linda: Yes, well, I guess I could go back and look that up, but . . .

Amy: [Putting on her suit jacket, gathering her briefcase, and leading Linda to the door] Glad I could help. Stop by Monday if you have any other questions.

Linda: [Realizing that Amy is going to leave] Wait! These questions are really important and will only take a few minutes! [Blocking the door with her body while riffling through a folder for the papers needed to ask the questions] Hold on a minute. I have everything right here.

Amy: [Very annoyed and angry] I don't have time to answer questions that you should have been able to answer by looking in your own workpapers. You also need to learn some manners and how to follow procedures around here. Now, please get out of my way or I'll call security! You should also be aware that I plan to meet with Jim to discuss your unprofessional behavior and ask him to have someone else assigned to our engagement.

Linda steps aside and stands speechless as Amy quickly walks past her to the elevator.

Writing task: Write a letter to Linda explaining why the interview was unsuccessful and suggesting what she could have done to make the meeting productive.

6. **Scenario:** Steve, warehouse manager, and Tom, staff auditor, just met to discuss the upcoming physical inventory count and observation. Their conversation was as follows:

Tom: Hi, Steve. Thanks for taking the time to meet with me.

Steve: No problem. Where shall we start?

Tom: Why don't you start by telling me how you've planned the physical count?

Steve: Sure. We've broken down the plant staff into two teams, A and B. Within each team, workers will be paired and assigned specific sections of the warehouse to count the stock. We've done it this way for the past two years and it's been really successful. For example, Pair 1 from Team A counts the first row of the warehouse. Later, Pair 1 from Team B will recount it to make sure the first count is accurate. If the teams disagree on the count, we get a supervisor to count it again to make a final determination.

Tom: Where is the more valuable inventory located?

Steve: The premier line goods are in the southeast corner. We've rearranged the location of goods since last year to improve warehouse operations and reduce losses from spoilage.

Tom: Has spoilage been a problem? And for that matter, what's your experience with obsolescence and theft of merchandise?

Steve: Whoa! No need to get alarmed! It's just that given the climate control and security systems we use, this was a better arrangement. It reduced our insurance costs, pilferage, and improved the flow of goods. Wish we would have thought of it sooner.

Tom: Fine, fine. [Mumbling more to himself than addressing this to Steve] We'll have to be really careful about this issue; there could be problems with inventory valuation. Definitely an increased risk all around.

Steve: What's that? Did you ask me something?

Tom: No, no. Sounds like you have a good grasp of this area. Is there anything else I need to know?

Steve: Not really. But I have some other information you might find helpful. Here's a map of the warehouse, listing of the pairs by team, inventory costing sheet, and schedule for the inventory count.

Tom: Thanks a lot. This is a great help. I'll see you on the 31st.

Writing task: Write a memo to the workpapers summarizing Tom and Steve's meeting. Structure the memo like a report and include an introduction, background description, explanation, and conclusion. Also include your opinion on the adequacy of the client's plan for counting the inventory.

7. **Scenario:** The following is an excerpt from the audit workpapers for Bob's Auto Repair.

Bob's Auto Repair
Bank Reconciliation
December 31, 2003

Balance per bank	$ 17,851.76	a
Plus: deposit in transit	2,222.56	b
Less: outstanding checks	($5,465.25)	c
Adjusted balance	$ 14,609.07	d
Balance per general ledger	$ 14,864.07	e
Less: bank service charges	(45.00)	f
Less: ISF check returned	(210.00)	g
Adjusted balance	$ 14,609.07	h

Tickmark Legend
a) Confirmed balance with bank; agrees with cutoff bank statement
b) Agrees with cutoff bank statement; traced to cash receipts journal; inspected copy of deposit slip
c) Traced to cash disbursements journal; examined checks returned with cutoff bank statement
d) Footed; agrees with general ledger
e) Agrees with general ledger balance
f) Agrees with December bank statement
g) Followed up on the disposition of this check
h) Footed; agrees with general ledger.

Writing task: Many of the tickmark explanations on this workpaper are incomplete, others are unclear, and some are duplicates. Revise the workpaper tickmarks and tickmark explanations for greater clarity and efficiency. Add information that you think is necessary to make the explanations clear.

8. **Scenario:** You are a first-year staff accountant assigned to Outlook Company's audit team. Your senior asked you to interview Outlook's treasurer, controller, and sales manager to obtain an understanding of their sales processing and credit approval procedures. Your goal was to understand this part of Outlook's accounting system clearly enough to be able to write the internal control narrative for these procedures for the audit workpapers. During your interviews you took the following notes.

   Controller's Information
   - Sales orders and invoices are prenumbered documents.
   - If credit is approved, the billing department gets the sales order and the customer purchase order from the credit manager.
   - Billing department prepares a sales invoice after it receives the sales order.
   - Sales invoice is a four-part form; two copies are kept with the sales order and the customer PO and put into a temporary file, pending shipment.
   - A third copy of the sales invoice goes to the shipping department and is filed in a temporary file until the goods are released from the warehouse.

   Sales Manager's Information
   - Salesclerks receive POs from customers from mailroom.
   - Phone orders are also taken by salesclerks (keep phone log).
   - After getting customer's order, salesclerks prepare a "sales order" that includes an estimate of the total price of the order.
   - Sales order goes to credit manager for approval.
   - Customers' POs (if received) are attached to the sales order by the salesclerks.

   Treasurer's Information
   - Credit approval based on a predetermined credit limit for each customer and current outstanding AR for that customer.
   - Credit manager signs the sales order if credit is approved.

   Writing task
   a. Write the internal control narrative for Outlook's sales processing and credit approval procedures handling based on your notes. Supplement your text with a flowchart.
   b. Write a memo to the senior summarizing any unanswered questions or areas that may require additional information.

9. **Scenario:** Jerry, the audit senior responsible for the Coffee-Time Company audit, has been given an emergency assignment and does not have time to write all of the management comment letter. Because you are the staff auditor with the most experience on the job, Jerry has asked you to draft the recommendations for operational improvement which, if implemented, will strengthen Coffee-Time's internal controls. The letter will be given directly to the partner in charge for her approval. Jerry has provided you with the following set of notes:

Information System Records
- All employees, including programmers, have access to computer programs and data files.

Capitalization of Plant and Equipment
- No formal policy for capitalization vs. expensing of acquisitions of PP&E; lots of inconsistencies—some acquisitions for $1,500 are expensed when they should be capitalized; others, purchased for as little as $300, are capitalized.

Bank Reconciliations
- Bank reconciliations are prepared by the same accounts payable clerk who prepares and signs checks; no review of reconciliations.

Writing task: For each of the three areas, draft comments suitable for inclusion in the management comment letter to Coffee-Time. Clearly describe what the company has been doing in each of these areas and what consequences will ensue if the problem is ignored. Also, explain the actions management could take to improve their system and the positive effects that your solution will bring.

10. **Scenario:** You are a staff auditor for Merck & Morgan, CPAs, and have just completed the year-end audit of Technology Unlimited, Inc. Doing business as Computers Unlimited, the company owns four stores in local strip malls and provides extensive customer service along with the computers and other high-tech equipment it sells. During the audit you discovered several weaknesses in the company's internal control and operations systems that are not material and do not constitute reportable conditions as defined by the AICPA, but nevertheless are situations that management might want to address to improve the company's operations and internal control structure.

- No management approval is required for a sales associate to override the system and give a percentage discount on merchandise that is not on sale.
- The accounting system does not distinguish between discounts for merchandise that is on sale (where the discount was approved by management) and discounts that are given by sales associates overriding the system.
- No password is required to gain access to the point-of-sale (POS) system (checkout computer and cash register).
- Although each sales associate is required to enter a unique ID into the POS system when ringing up a sale, the IDs are commonly known by everyone since they are printed on each receipt.
- When an employee is terminated, it may take several weeks for the human resources department to complete paperwork and remove the employee's ID from the system.

Communication task: Prepare a management comment letter for Technology Unlimited, Inc., that includes suggestions for improving the weaknesses described. Use the Observation and Management Action format discussed in the guide. Be sure to explain why each weakness in the current system poses a problem and how your suggestion will strengthen the company's internal controls. Make up any additional facts you need to prepare a well-written letter.

Exercises 11 through 17 relate to the following audit scenario:

WILCO IN TROUBLE*

Client Background

You are an audit senior at Andrews, Keller, and Baskin, a public accounting firm. You have been assigned to the audit of Wilco Corporation for the current year. Wilco Corporation is a publicly traded manufacturer of computer chips.

Wilco has been a good audit client of the firm for the past six years, paying bills on a time, employing cooperative management, and complying with authoritative accounting pronouncements. During those years, however, Wilco has been losing market share in an increasingly competitive global marketplace. Although Wilco's unit sales have been increasing each year, they drastically lag behind industry increases. Currently, stagnation in the computer chip and router markets is significantly reducing the market demand for Wilco's chips. Wilco's stock has declined in value from approximately $95 per share in 1997 to $48 per share in 2003.

Despite these downward trends, Wilco remains a widely recognized name in the computer chip market.

Planning Meeting

At the instruction of the engagement partner, you will hold a planning meeting with Samantha Strong, CEO, to discuss current year events and plan the strategy for the upcoming audit. In your meeting, Samantha indicates that Wilco is going to have a very good year, despite some difficulties in the recent past. The company's main difficulty has involved revocation of its line of credit: As a result of lower-than-expected sales volume last year, Wilco violated its bank debt covenants, and the bank refused to renew the line of credit. Samantha indicates, however, that a new discount policy, encouraging customers to pay on a more timely basis, has increased cash flow, and operations have not been hampered despite the lack of credit from the bank.

Samantha further indicates that in May of the current year, Jane Smith, CFO, resigned to pursue other opportunities. Jane was replaced as chief financial officer by Samantha's close personal friend, Jonathan White. Samantha praises Jonathan's mastery of accounting and reporting, commending his ability to record financial transactions in ways that more accurately reflect the operations of the business than Jane's methods had. Samantha feels that Jonathan's philosophy is more practical than Jane's "overly conservative" approach to accounting. "Jonathan's logical approach to recording transactions and his ability to record results that better reflect our performance is doing wonders for our business. Just knowing that we were doing things so wrong in the past has bothered me tremendously," Samantha states.

Samantha indicates that one of Wilco's major suppliers went on strike during June and July of the current year. During this strike, Wilco was forced to buy parts from another supplier at significantly higher costs. Nevertheless, Samantha explains, the bottom line did not suffer. The new CFO performed a study of the overhead application process and redistributed items that were incorrectly accounted for in the past. Due to the lower overhead costs, Samantha expects product cost to be significantly lower after the month of July than in prior years. She explains: "Despite the increase in product cost for those two months, we experienced no negative gross profit impact because Jonathan reworked the overhead formula to reflect overhead costs more accurately. In fact, our products are significantly cheaper than we thought. Now we can reduce sales prices and increase volume due to more competitive pricing."

Samantha says that no other significant events occurred this year. She mentions a few minor items, such as the purchase of a significant amount of fixed assets and a growth in the customer base as a result of a new credit granting policy.

While discussing your planning meeting with the audit partner, you note the following concerns and areas of risk:

- Management's integrity (specifically the CFO)—the drastic improvement in current year results
- Inventory Valuation—the new overhead application formula
- Propriety of Cost of Goods Sold—the new overhead application formula
- Possibility of a going concern issue—lack of bank funding
- Valuation of reserves and liabilities
- Potential risk of loss—new credit granting policy.

Audit Fieldwork

Sales/Cost of Sales

In performing your regression analysis of sales and cost of goods sold, you note that, according to prior year workpapers, gross profit rates have averaged between 38% and 41% over the past six years. The client provided the following data for the analysis:

Month	Sales	COGS	Gross Profit
January	14,534,672	8,867,134	38.99%
February	15,068,010	9,063,465	39.85%
March	14,835,456	8,968,979	39.54%
April	14,236,726	8,613,564	39.50%
May	15,255,664	8,974,685	41.17%
June	14,365,790	8,313,646	42.13%
July	15,489,454	9,016,465	41.79%
August	14,964,889	8,065,646	46.10%
September	15,032,469	8,074,656	46.29%
October	17,028,646	8,765,646	48.52%
November	18,900,644	9,564,698	49.39%
December	19,365,471	9,679,879	50.01%
TOTAL	**$189,077,891**	**$105,968,463**	

In reviewing the data provided by the client, you note that sales increased significantly in the last three months of the year. Additionally, you note that gross profit margins increased beginning in August and further increased beginning in October. Discussions with Richard Jones, accounting manager, indicate the following:

- Profit margins would have increased beginning in June, but the strike affected the cost of direct materials used in production.
- The cost-of-goods-sold formula was altered to exclude insurance, depreciation, and sales salaries. Richard indicated that such items were excluded from overhead because they are paid for and utilized by nonproduction departments.

- Overtime paid to production workers is now recorded in the Human Resources Department as a fringe benefit. Such cost has historically been tracked in the production department and included as a component of cost of goods sold. Jonathan, the CFO, changed this policy under the rationale that this overtime premium is given by the Human Resources Department as part of the new contract and should therefore be a Human Resources expense (recorded as administrative expense on the income statement), not includable as a component of cost of sales. This policy went into effect in October.

- A promotion went into effect in October whereby Wilco sold bulk quantities of computer chips to a significant number of customers. Wilco is trying to promote the use of its products by having them readily available in bulk to customers. Wilco shipped these additional quantities to customers in good faith along with their regular orders. In a letter to customers, Wilco said, "We want to be the supplier of choice for computer chips. Please accept these chips for use in your production needs. If you do not need or use them, you may return them within three months with no obligation." Wilco recorded the sale of goods and the related account receivable upon shipment.

Fixed Asset Additions and Disposals

Remembering Samantha's statement that considerable fixed assets were purchased this year, you ask Joseph Danna, fixed asset clerk, about the nature of these fixed assets. Joseph indicates that a significant portion of the fixed asset additions represent labor by company mechanics. Such labor was incurred during a routine two-week plant shutdown in which each machine was thoroughly cleaned and inspected by the maintenance department. Additionally, plant walkways and work areas were resurfaced. Joseph tells you that these costs were capitalized because they enhance the useful lives of the machinery and equipment. Additionally, all replacement parts bought during the year for these machines (nuts, bolts, compressors, arms, etc.) were capitalized because they become part of the fixed asset.

When you ask Joseph why these labor and replacement costs were treated as fixed assets, he replies that Jonathan, the CFO, ordered the change from the previous capitalization policy. Joseph assures you that the policy is correct because these items and labor costs are related to fixed assets and should be capitalized. Continuing your discussion of fixed assets, you ask whether any disposals occurred during the current year. Joseph is not aware of any; however, such disposals occur at the discretion of the plant managers and are not brought to the attention of the accounting department.

Credit Granting Policy

While talking to Richard Jones, accounting manager, you learn that Wilco is relaxing the guidelines by which credit is granted. In the past, only the credit manager could approve credit. Now, however, credit approvals have been decentralized: Each credit clerk is responsible for a region of the market, authorized to grant credit for that region, without credit manager approvals. Additionally, clerks are responsible for determining bad debt write-offs and recoveries for their own region based on whether or not, in their professional judgment, they feel that collection will be made. This policy change—decentralizing the credit granting function—was initiated to empower the employees and create a greater sense of participation in management.

Conclusion

When you complete your audit fieldwork, you report your progress to the engagement partner, Steve Smart. Although net income has increased significantly in the current year and outpaced the industry average, the audit partner is uneasy with this increase. Steve is concerned that the company's sales policy is too aggressive and its accounting for certain sales is possibly not in accordance with GAAP. Additionally, Steve is not sure whether the company's overhead policies follow procedures recommended under GAAP. Both you and Steve are uncertain about the entity's ability to continue as a going concern, and about Andrews, Keller, and Baskin's ability to issue an unqualified opinion without significant adjustment to the financial statements.

11. Write an audit-planning memorandum.
12. Write tickmark explanations describing the reasons for changes in gross profit percentages. Indicate whether or not the changes are justified with regard to overhead application.
13. Write a memo to the workpapers indicating whether you think Wilco's cost of goods sold policy is acceptable.
14. Write a memo to the workpapers indicating whether the client's sales policy is in accordance with the guidelines of FASB 48, Revenue Recognition.
15. Write a memo to the audit partner describing the client's new fixed asset additions policy and whether or not you feel that such policy is in accordance with GAAP.
16. Write a workpaper supporting your position about whether or not a going concern issue exists regarding Wilco.
17. Write a management comment letter to the board of directors of Wilco indicating any inefficiencies, weaknesses in internal control, or recommendations you may have to improve the accounting operations of Wilco.

*The comprehensive audit engagement exercise "Wilco in Trouble" was prepared by Ryan R. Fox.